SIGHT READING & RHYTHM EVERY DAY®

Helen Marlais with Kevin Olson

| DAY ONE 1 | DAY TWO 2 | DAY THREE 3 | DAY FOUR 4 | DAY FIVE 5 |

★ LESSON DAY

T H E
F·J·H
MUSIC
COMPANY
I N C.
Frank J. Hackinson

(800) 876-9777
10075 SW Beav-Hills Hwy (503) 641-5091
1010 SE Powell (503) 775-0800
12334 SE Division (503) 760-6881

Production: Frank J. Hackinson
Production Coordinators: Philip Groeber and Isabel Otero Bowen
Cover: Terpstra Design, San Francisco
Text Design and Layout: Terpstra Design and Maritza Cosano Gomez
Engraving: Kevin Olson and Tempo Music Press, Inc.
Printer: Tempo Music Press, Inc.

ISBN-13: 978-1-56939-474-8

ABOUT THE AUTHORS

Helen Marlais' active performance schedule includes concerts in North America, Western and Eastern Europe, the Middle East, and Asia, and her travels abroad have included performing and teaching at the leading conservatories in Lithuania, Estonia, Italy, France, Hungary, Turkey, Russia, China, and England. She has performed with members of the Pittsburgh, Minnesota, Grand Rapids, Des Moines, Cedar Rapids, and Beijing National Symphony Orchestras to name a few, and is recorded on Stargrass Records®, Gasparo, and Centaur record labels. She has had numerous collaborative performances broadcast regionally, nationally, and internationally on radio, television, and the Internet with her husband, clarinetist Arthur Campbell. She presents workshops at every national convention and is a featured presenter at state conventions. She has been a guest teacher and performer at leading music schools and conservatories throughout North America, Europe, and Asia. Dr. Marlais is the Director of Keyboard Publications for The FJH Music Company Inc. Her articles can be read in *Keyboard Companion, The American Music Teacher,* and *Clavier* magazines.

Dr. Marlais is an associate professor of piano at Grand Valley State University in Grand Rapids, Michigan, where she directs the piano pedagogy program, coordinates the group piano programs, and teaches studio piano. She received her DM in piano performance and pedagogy from Northwestern University and her MM in piano performance from Carnegie Mellon University. She has also held full-time faculty piano positions at the Crane School of Music, S.U.N.Y. at Potsdam, Iowa State University, and Gustavus Adolphus College. Visit: www.helenmarlais.com.

Kevin Olson is an active pianist, composer, and faculty member at Elmhurst College near Chicago, Illinois, where he teaches classical and jazz piano, music theory, and electronic music. He holds a Doctor of Education degree from National-Louis University, and bachelor's and master's degrees in music composition and theory from Brigham Young University. Before teaching at Elmhurst College, he held a visiting professor position at Humboldt State University in California.

A native of Utah, Kevin began composing at the age of five. When he was twelve, his composition *An American Trainride* received the Overall First Prize at the 1983 National PTA Convention in Albuquerque, New Mexico. Since then, he has been a composer-in- residence at the National Conference on Piano Pedagogy and has written music for the American Piano Quartet, Chicago a cappella, the Rich Matteson Jazz Festival, and several piano teachers associations around the country.

Kevin maintains a large piano studio, teaching students of a variety of ages and abilities. Many of the needs of his own piano students have inspired a diverse collection of books and solos published by The FJH Music Company Inc., which he joined as a writer in 1994.

HOW THE SERIES IS ORGANIZED

All rhythmic activities

All sight-reading activities

Place a ✔ when you have been successful!

Each unit of the series is divided into five separate days of enjoyable rhythmic and sight-reading activities. Students complete these short activities "Every Day" at home, by themselves. Every Day the words, "Did It!" are found in a box for the student to check once they have completed both the rhythm and sight-reading activities.

The new concepts are identified in the upper right-hand corner of each unit. Once introduced, these concepts are continually reinforced through subsequent units.

On the lesson day, there are short rhythmic and sight-reading activities that will take only minutes for the teacher and student to do together. An enjoyable sight-reading duet wraps up each unit.

BOOKS 1A AND 1B

Rhythm:

The first unit in book 1B incorporates UNIT counting. UNIT counting (♩ ♩ ♩) is beneficial because the student learns the exact rhythmic pulse of each particular note. When students have a firm grasp of unit counting, they can easily make the transition to METRIC counting (♩ ♩ ♩ ♩), which is counting the number of beats in a measure.

The teacher may decide which counting system to use throughout the book, although unit counting is extremely beneficial at the earliest stages of music making.

Rhythmic activities in books 1A/B include the following:

- Students are asked to count rhythmic examples out loud and clap, tap, point, and march.
- Students learn directional reading.
- Students speak lyrics in rhythm.
- Students add bar lines to excerpts and then count the rhythmic examples out loud.
- Students are asked to pulse with their feet and march in step, to feel a constant pulse.
- Students are asked to clap rhythmic examples by memory, an excellent ear training and memory exercise.
- Students tap different rhythms in both hands.
- Students learn and drill ²₄, ³₄, and ⁴₄, time signatures.

Fingering:

In book 1A, alternate fingering is provided so that students learn to play patterns starting on other fingers instead of always resorting to the thumb. In book 1B, very little fingering is provided so that students learn to look ahead and think about patterns.

Reading:

Students start the series by recognizing the following guide notes: treble G, bass F, and middle C (both clefs). After that, they read patterns starting a second above or below these guide notes. Students then progress into sight-reading patterns starting on guide notes an octave above and below middle C. This is followed by patterns starting a third above or below all of the guide notes, then a fourth above or below all of the guide notes they have learned up to this point.

The keys of C, G, F, D, and A major are learned in books 1A and 1B, as well as the intervals of harmonic and melodic seconds, thirds, fourths, and fifths.

Sight Reading activities include the following:

- The student learns to "plan" for note and rhythmic accuracy, correct articulations, and a good sound.
- Helpful suggestions guide students to think before they play, and not stop once they have started!
- Students are asked to sing the melody of some of the excerpts, which encourages them to listen while maintaining a constant pulse and the forward motion of the musical line.
- Students circle and analyze intervals and patterns before playing.
- The metronome is incorporated once a week.

Developing these important skills lays the proper foundation for music making and fosters stellar piano playing. A student who sight reads well has the skills to progress rapidly and enjoy success. *Sight Reading & Rhythm Every Day*® is a sure way to produce the positive results that motivate students.

FJH153

TABLE OF CONTENTS

Unit 11

New Concept: $\frac{2}{4}$ time signature

 Rhythm—Clap the following rhythmic examples and whisper the counting!

DID IT!

Place a ✔ when you have been successful!

1.

| Unit Counting: | 1 – 2 | 1 | 1 | 1 – 2 | 1 – 2 | 1 | 1 | 1 – 2 |
| Metric Counting: | 1 – 2 | 1 – 2 | 1 – 2 | 1 – 2 | 1 – 2 | 1 – 2 |

2.

 Sight reading—Tap and count the rhythm before playing.
Then play the melody without stopping, always looking ahead.

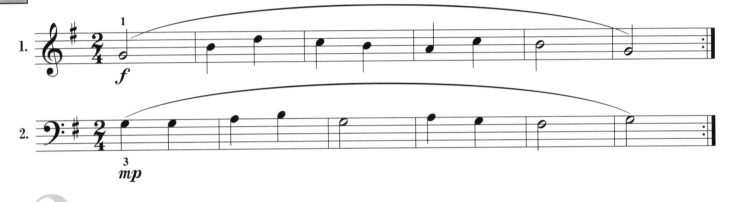

 Rhythm—Draw arrows (up or down) to show the direction of the musical line, and circle each group of repeated notes. Point to each note as you count along.

DID IT!

1.

2.

 Sight reading—Clap and count the melodies. Then play with energy!

6

Rhythm—Speak the lyrics in rhythm while you point to each note.

DID IT!

1. Jump - ing   on   the   tramp - o - line,   Bounce!   Bounce!

2. Snail,   why   are   you   so   slow?

Sight reading—Tap the rhythm before playing. Play and sing the melody, and don't stop!

Rhythm—Add bar lines to the following rhythms.
When you have finished, clap and count each line twice.

DID IT!

Sight reading—Clap and count each melody line before playing.
Can you clap the rhythm of each example a second time without looking at the music?

DAY FIVE

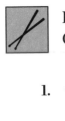 Rhythm—Tap the following rhythmic examples.
Count loudly with energy in your voice!

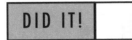

 Sight reading—With the metronome set at ♩ = 80, clap or tap the following examples.
Then play these at the same metronome speed.

 Rhythm—Point to the example you hear your teacher clap. Listen carefully!
Then clap and count both examples.

 Sight reading—Point to the melody you hear your teacher play. Can you sing it?
Then choose an example to play for your teacher.

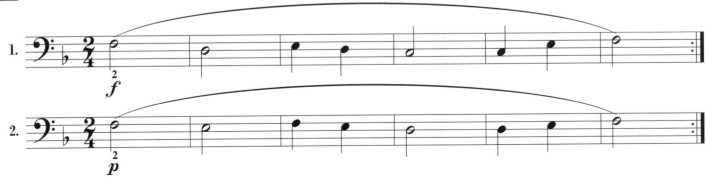

FJH1530

Ensemble Piece

DID IT!

Before you begin this duet, point to the notes and count the rhythm of the piece. Keep your eyes on the music and count as you play. Would a *Country Hoedown* be cheerful or sad?

Country Hoedown

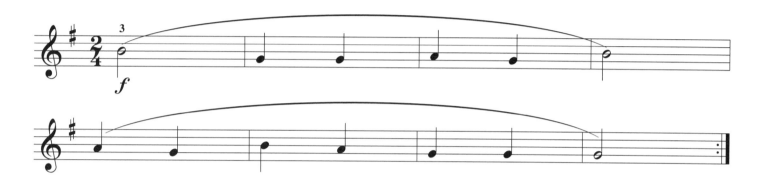

Teacher accompaniment (student plays as written)

? After playing, ask yourself, "Did this duet sound like a Hoedown?"

Unit 12

2/20/12   articulation

New Concepts: harmonic fifths; *staccato*; key signature of D major

DAY ONE

 Rhythm—Clap the following rhythmic examples and count out loud!

DID IT! ✓

 1.

 2.

 Sight reading—Circle the harmonic fifths before playing. Silently play the musical examples on the fallboard preparing the F sharps, and thinking about the *staccato* and *legato* articulations.

D Major

DAY TWO

3/6/13

 **Rhythm**—Draw arrows (up or down) to show the direction of the musical line, and circle each group of repeated notes. Point to each note as you count along.

DID IT! ✓

 Sight reading—Plan ahead: key signature, tempo, fingering, and articulations. Feel the pulse of the rhythm as you play.

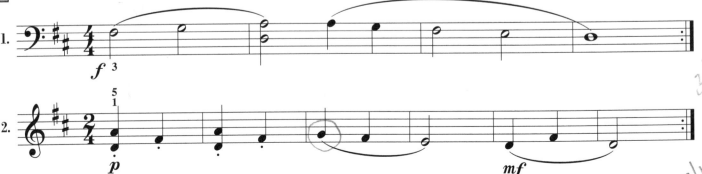

FJH153

DAY THREE

Rhythm—Speak the lyrics in rhythm while you point to each note.

DID IT! ✓

1. Watch as I play each dy - nam - ic with ease.

2. Eyes on the mu - sic! Don't peek at your hands!

Sight reading—Tap the rhythm before playing. Counting *while you play* will help you keep a steady beat.

DAY FOUR 3/6/13

fun!!!

Rhythm—Add bar lines to the following rhythms.
When you have finished, stand up and stomp these rhythms with your feet!

DID IT! ✓

Sight reading—Silently play these melodies on the top of the keys. Observe the articulations.
Then play at a tempo that you can keep steady.

3/28/13

3/20/13

D Major

11

 3/20/13

DAY FIVE

 Rhythm—Tap the following rhythmic examples.
Count out loud with confidence!

DID IT! ✓

 Sight reading—With the metronome set at ♩ = 80, clap or tap the following examples.
Then play these melodies at the same metronome speed.

★ **LESSON DAY** 3/20/13

 Rhythm—Point to the rhythm you hear your teacher clap. Then choose an example to clap.
Can you clap either example from memory?

 Sight reading—Your teacher will play one of the following melodies.
Decide which one you hear. Then sight read both examples.

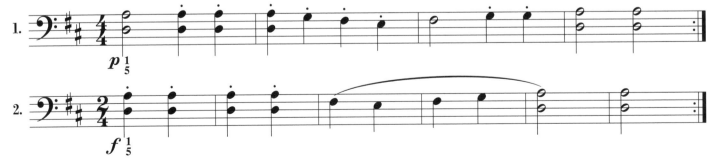

FJH1530

Ensemble Piece

DID IT!

Before you begin this duet, tap and count the rhythm of the student part. In order for *Distant Drums* to be effective, the rhythm must be steady. Keep your eyes on the music and count as you play.

Distant Drums

Teacher accompaniment (student plays as written)

? After playing, ask yourself, "Did I play this piece with a steady, drumming beat?"

Unit 13

New Concepts: harmonic thirds;
guide notes—treble and bass C

DAY ONE

 Rhythm—Clap the following rhythmic examples and count with energy!   **DID IT!**

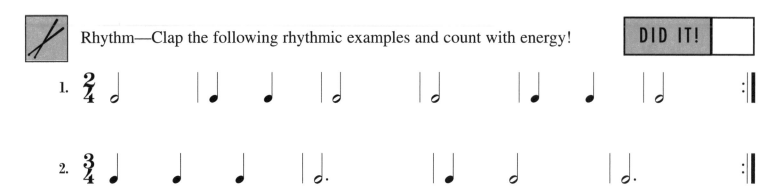

Sight reading—Plan ahead: circle the guide notes of treble C and bass C. Circle the harmonic thirds. Clap and count the examples. Play with a big, warm sound. Then play again, adding the dynamics.

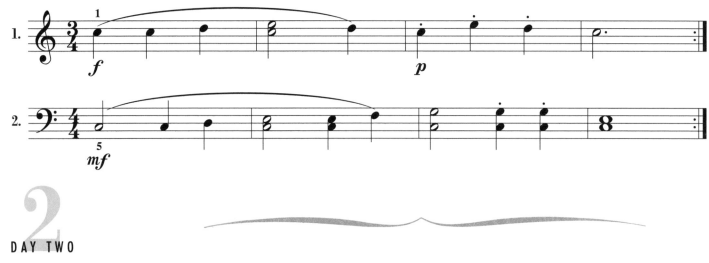

DAY TWO

Rhythm—Draw arrows (up or down) to show the direction of the musical line, and circle each group of repeated notes. Point to each note as you count along.   **DID IT!**

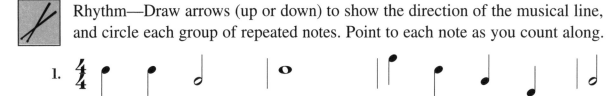

Sight reading—1) Play all the harmonic thirds. 2) Clap and count the melodies. 3) Then play with confidence!

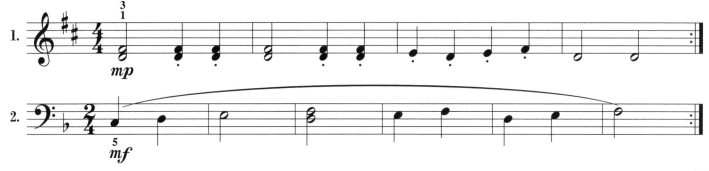

14

FJH1536

3
DAY THREE

Rhythm—Speak the lyrics in rhythm while you point to each note.

DID IT!

1. 4/4

I rode the rol - ler - coast - er twen - ty times 'til I got sick!

2. 2/4

Can you hear the wood - peck - er tap a stead - y beat?

Sight reading—Circle all of the harmonic thirds. Silently play these melodies on the top of the keys at ♩ = 84. Then play the examples while keeping a steady beat!

1. *mf*

2. *f*

4
DAY FOUR

Rhythm—Add bar lines to the following rhythms.
When you have finished, clap the rhythms while marching to the beat!

DID IT!

1. 4/4

2. 3/4

Sight reading—Circle all of the harmonic fifths before playing.
Play slowly enough so that you do not stop.

1. *mf*

2. *mp*

 Rhythm—Tap the following rhythmic examples.
Count loudly with energy in your voice!

1.

2.

 Sight reading—Silently play these melodies on top of the keys at ♩ = 116.
Keep a steady beat while you play, and listen to the rise and fall of the melody.

1.

2.

 LESSON DAY

 Rhythm—Clap and count one of the following rhythmic examples for your teacher.
First clap it slowly, then once quickly. Decide with your teacher if your clapping was steady!

1.

2.

 Sight reading—Circle all of the harmonic fifths in each example below. Find the fifths on the piano, then
do the same with all of the harmonic thirds. Then play both examples at a tempo that you can keep steady!

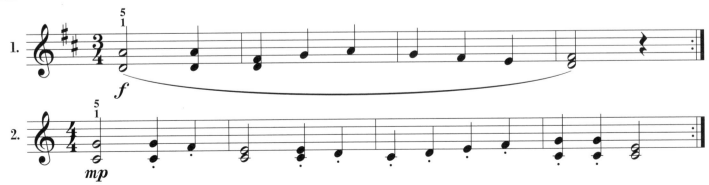

FJH1530

Ensemble Piece

Before you begin this duet, clap and count the rhythm of the student part. What fingers will you use for the harmonic fifths at the beginning of the piece? Keep your eyes on the music and count as you play!

Angel's Song

Teacher accompaniment (student plays one octave higher)

After playing, ask yourself, "Did the piece sound angelic?"

Unit 14

New Concept: harmonic seconds

DAY ONE

Rhythm—Clap the following rhythmic examples and count with confidence!

DID IT! ☐

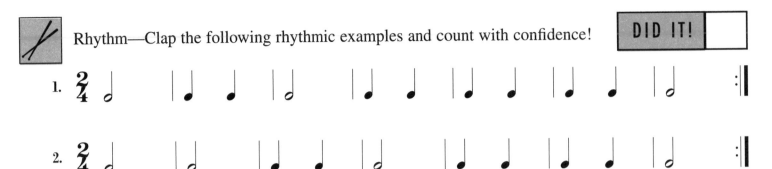

Sight reading—Circle all of the harmonic seconds. Tap and count the rhythm before playing. Play the examples without stopping, keeping your eyes on the music.

DAY TWO

Rhythm—Draw arrows (up or down) to show the direction of the musical line, and circle each group of repeated notes. Point to each note as you count along.

DID IT! ☐

Sight reading—Count the rhythm of these melodies silently while following the music with your eyes. Plan the sound and articulations before playing!

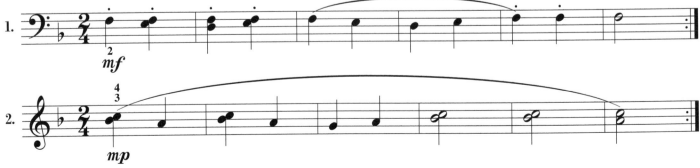

FJH1534

3
DAY THREE

Rhythm—Speak the lyrics in rhythm while you point to each note.

DID IT! ☐

1. I get to go to a birth - day par - ty!

2. Sat - ur - day morn - ings, I like to watch car - toons.

 Sight reading—Tap the rhythm before playing. Play all of the harmonic seconds, thirds, and fifths. Set a strong rhythmic pulse and you will be ready to play!

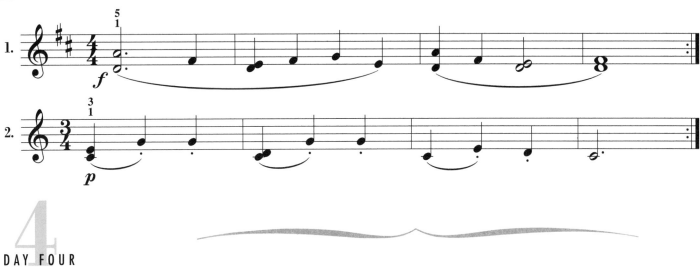

4
DAY FOUR

 Rhythm—Add bar lines to the following rhythms.
When you have finished, stand up and stomp these rhythms with your feet!

DID IT! ☐

1.

2.

Sight reading—Silently play these melodies on the top of the keys.
Then plan the sound and play out loud.

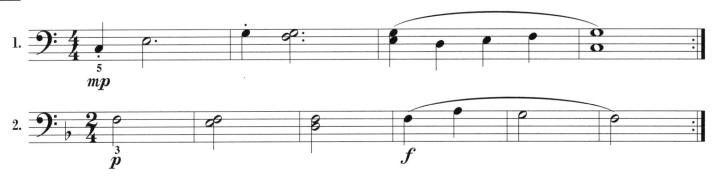

Rhythm—Tap the following rhythmic examples.
Count out loud with confidence!

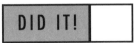

 Sight reading—Silently play these melodies on the top of the keys at ♩ = 76.
Keep a steady beat while you play and observe the articulations. Plan the sound before beginning!

★ LESSON DAY

 Rhythm—Add in the missing notes to make sure each measure is accurate.
Then tap both of them as you count.

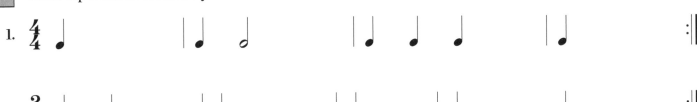

 Sight reading—Circle all of the harmonic seconds in each example below.
How are these examples similar/different? Listen for a steady pulse as you play each one.

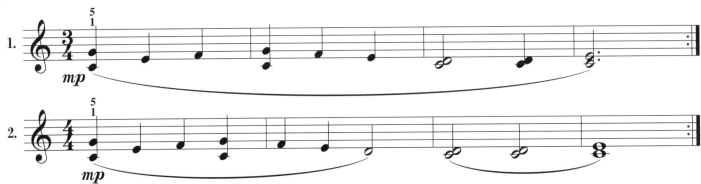

FJH1536

Ensemble Piece

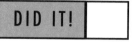

Before you begin this duet, clap and count the rhythm of the student part. Keep your eyes on the music and count as you play.

Popcorn Popper

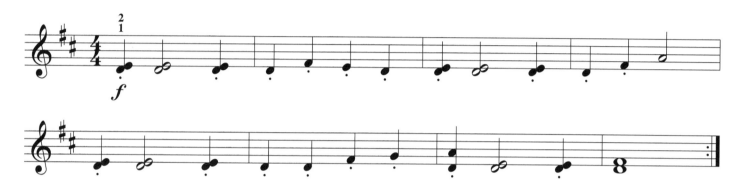

Teacher accompaniment (student plays one octave higher than written)

? After playing, ask yourself, "Did the *staccato* notes pop?"

Unit 15

New Concepts: harmonic fourths; quarter rests

DAY ONE

 Rhythm—Clap the following rhythmic examples and whisper the rests!

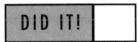

 Sight reading—Before playing, count while pointing to each beat.
Circle all of the harmonic fourths. Then play with a strong rhythmic pulse!

DAY TWO

 Rhythm—Draw arrows (up or down) to show the direction of the musical line, and circle each group of repeated notes. Point to each note as you count along.

 Sight reading—Prepare yourself by looking over the rhythm and the key of these examples. Plan the fingering and the articulations. Then play with confidence, and don't stop!

FJH1536

3 DAY THREE

Rhythm—Speak the lyrics in rhythm while you point to each note.

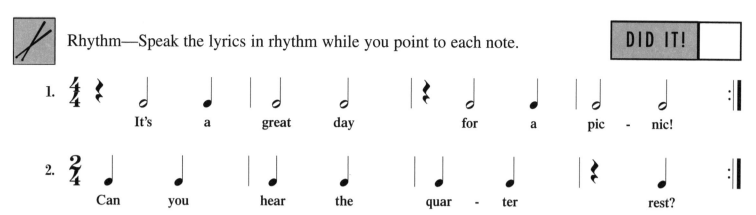

1. It's a great day for a pic - nic!

2. Can you hear the quar - ter rest?

Sight reading—Before playing, tap the rhythm and silently play all of the harmonic intervals.

4 DAY FOUR

Rhythm—Add bar lines to the following rhythms.
Clap the examples twice, the second time faster than the first!

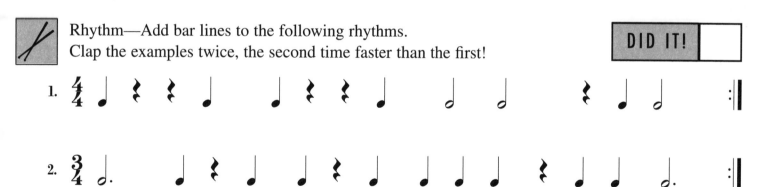

Sight reading—Circle all of the harmonic fourths below. Silently and steadily play the examples on the top of the keys. When you think you can play these examples perfectly, go ahead and play out loud!

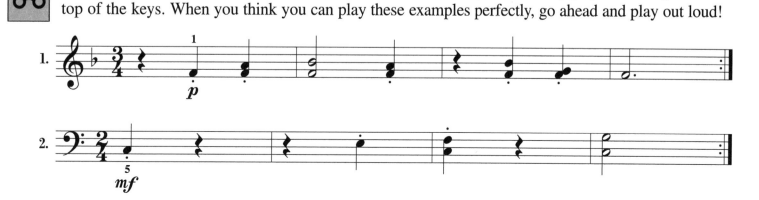

DAY FIVE

 Rhythm—Tap the following rhythmic examples.
Count loudly with energy in your voice!

 Sight reading—With the metronome set at ♩ = 92, clap or tap the following examples.
Then play them at the same metronome speed. Repeat the process at ♩ = 104.

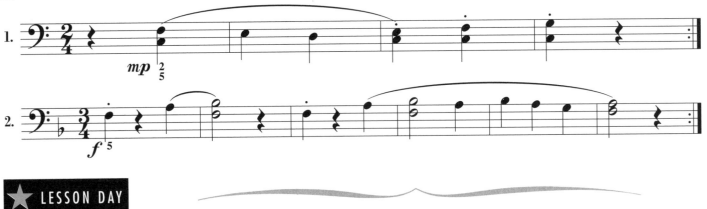

⭐ LESSON DAY

 Rhythm—Tap the top line while your teacher taps the bottom line. Then switch parts!

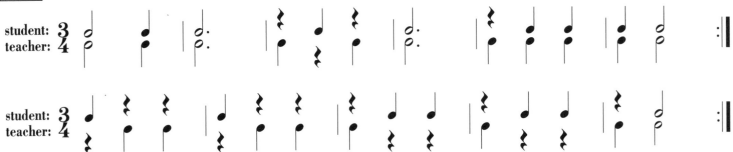

 Sight reading—Circle the harmonic fourths in the examples below and find them on the piano.
Listen for a *legato* sound in the first example and a *staccato* sound in the second example.

FJH1536

Ensemble Piece

Before you begin this duet, clap and count the rhythm of the student part. Whisper all of the rests. Decide if the intervals are harmonic seconds, thirds, fourths, or fifths. Imagine you are listening to bagpipes—perhaps the musician is playing at the top of a mountain in Scotland.

Scottish Bagpipes

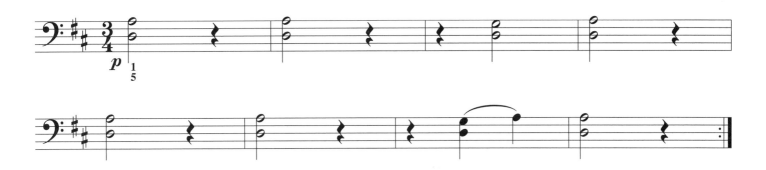

Teacher accompaniment (student plays one octave lower than written)

? After playing, ask yourself, "Did this piece sound like bagpipes played in the distance?"

Unit 16

DAY ONE

Rhythm—Clap the following rhythmic examples and count with energy!
Whisper the rests.

Sight reading—Look at the first note of both examples and mark the closest guide note (middle C, bass F, treble G, treble C, or bass C) that is a third away. Feel the pulse of the rhythm as you play.

DAY TWO

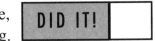

Rhythm—Draw arrows (up or down) to show the direction of the musical line, and circle each group of repeated notes. Point to each note as you count along.

Sight reading—Plan ahead! Look at the time and key signatures, fingering, and articulations. Play at a slow tempo that you can keep steady!

FJH1536

3
DAY THREE

Rhythm—Speak the lyrics in rhythm while you point to each note.

DID IT!

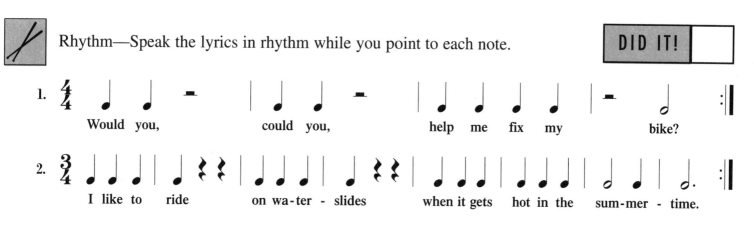

Would you,   could you,   help me fix my   bike?

I like to ride   on wa-ter - slides   when it gets   hot in the   sum-mer - time.

Sight reading—Tap the rhythm before playing. Look at the first note of each example and mark the closest guide note (middle C, treble G, bass F, treble C, or bass C) that is a third away. Decide how you want each example to sound before playing!

4
DAY FOUR

Rhythm—Add bar lines to the following rhythms.
When you have finished, clap and count each line twice.

DID IT!

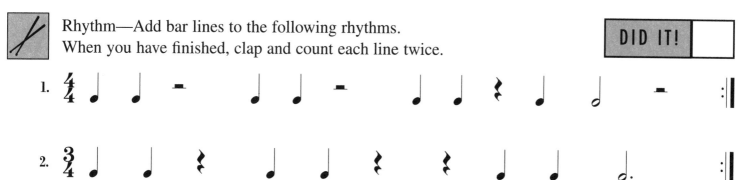

Sight reading—Silently play these melodies on the top of the keys. Be sure to always look ahead!

Rhythm—Tap the following rhythmic examples.
Count loudly with energy in your voice!

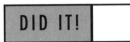

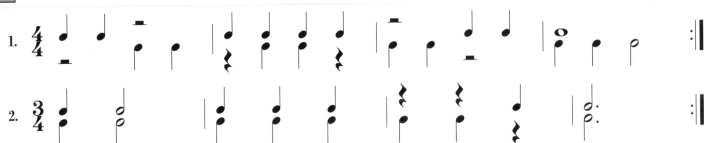

 Sight reading—With the metronome set at ♩ = 120, clap or tap the following examples.
Then play these at the same metronome speed. If you make a mistake, keep going!

★ LESSON DAY

 Rhythm—From each of the following rhythmic examples, create a melody using the
F major 5-finger scale.

 Sight reading—How are the examples below similar/different?
When you play them, don't forget the F sharps!

28

Ensemble Piece

Before you begin this duet, clap and count the rhythm of the student part. Circle all of the harmonic thirds. Keep your eyes on the music and keep it steady as you play.

At the Carnival

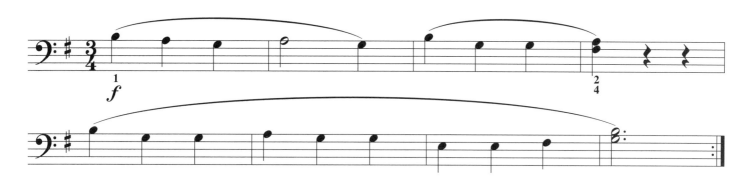

Teacher accompaniment (student plays as written)

? After playing, ask yourself, "Can I imagine a merry-go-round when I play this piece?"

Unit 17

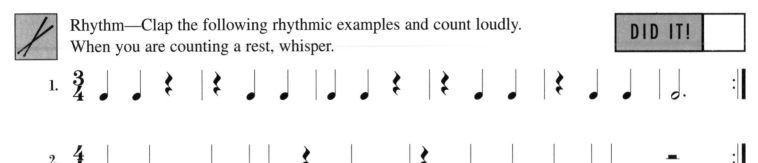

New Concepts: ◁ and ▷;
key signature of A major

DAY ONE

Rhythm—Clap the following rhythmic examples and count loudly.
When you are counting a rest, whisper.

DID IT!

Sight reading—Tap and count the rhythm before playing. Both melodies are in A major so place your
fingers over the notes of the A major 5-finger scale. Then play the examples without stopping!

DAY TWO

Rhythm—Draw arrows (up or down) to show the direction of the musical line,
and circle each group of repeated notes. Point to each note as you count along.

DID IT!

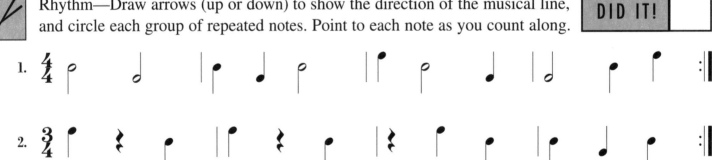

Sight reading—Clap and count these examples. Then play with energy, observing all the
articulations and rests! Can you hum the melody of example 2?

30

3 DAY THREE

Rhythm—Speak the lyrics in rhythm while you point to each note.

DID IT!

1. (4/4) Al - li - ga - tors all a - round! Run and hide, or you'll be found!

2. (3/4) I like to sit out - side in the sum-mer watch-ing the fi-re-flies light the night.

Sight reading—Tap the rhythm before playing.
Counting while you play will help you keep a steady beat.

1. mp < f

2. f mp

4 DAY FOUR

Rhythm—Add bar lines to the following rhythms.
Then stand and march the rhythms of each example!

DID IT!

1. 3/4

2. 4/4

Sight reading—Clap and count each example before playing. Can you clap the rhythm of each example without looking at the music?

1. mp f

2. p mf

Rhythm—Tap the following rhythmic examples.
Count out loud with confidence!

DID IT!

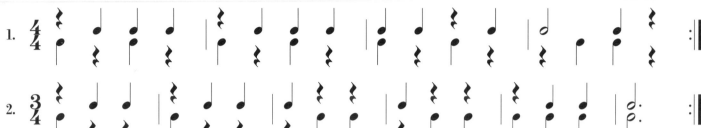

 Sight reading—With the metronome set at ♩ = 92, clap or tap the following examples.
Then play them at the same metronome speed. Repeat the process at ♩ = 104.

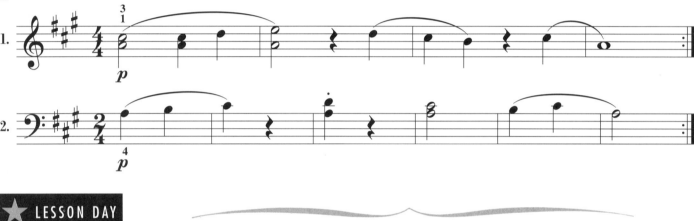

★ LESSON DAY

 Rhythm—Tap each example as a canon—start each line, and your teacher will tap the same line
one measure behind you. Then have your teacher begin the line, and begin tapping one measure later.

 Sight reading—Point to the example you hear your teacher play.
Then choose an example to sight read for your teacher.

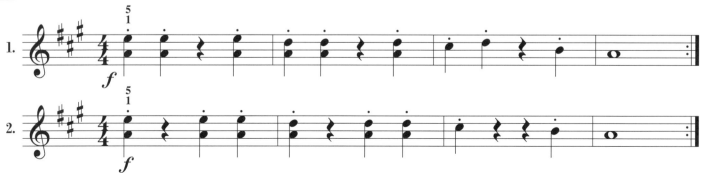

FJH1536

Ensemble Piece

DID IT!

Before you begin this duet, clap and count the rhythm of the student part. Block the melodic thirds (play them together) with a *f* sound. Keep your eyes on the music and count as you play.

Puppy Parade

Teacher accompaniment (student plays as written)

? After playing, ask yourself, "Did I bring out the *crescendo* in measures 5 and 6?"

Unit 18

New Concepts: melodic fourths starting
above or below the guide notes

1 DAY ONE

Rhythm—Clap the following rhythmic examples and count with confidence!   DID IT! ☐

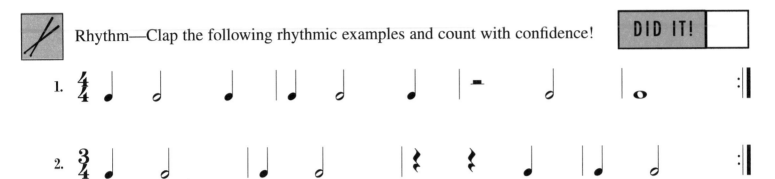

Sight reading—Circle and block (play together) all of the melodic fourths.
Decide the key. Then play as written at a steady tempo!

2 DAY TWO

 Rhythm—Draw arrows (up or down) to show the direction of the musical line,
and circle each group of repeated notes. Point to each note as you count along.   DID IT! ☐

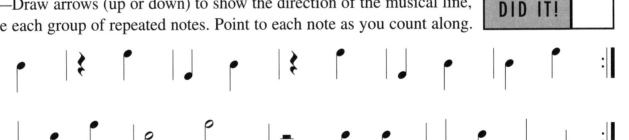

 Sight reading—Plan before playing. Look at the time and key signatures, fingering, intervals,
and articulations. Play and sing the melodies, and don't stop!

34

FJH1530

3
DAY THREE

Rhythm—Speak the lyrics in rhythm while you point to each note.

DID IT! ☐

1. Watch me blow the can - dles on my birth - day cake!

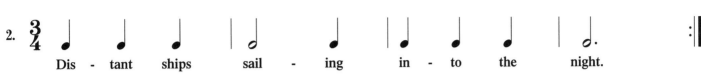

2. Dis - tant ships sail - ing in - to the night.

Sight reading—Tap the rhythm before playing. Decide if the melody goes up or down by seconds, thirds, or fourths. Circle all of the fourths. Then play each example with a strong rhythmic pulse.

4
DAY FOUR

Rhythm—Add bar lines to the following rhythms.
Then tap the rhythms on your lap, accenting each downbeat.

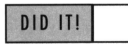 DID IT! ☐

Sight reading—Plan ahead: Study the rhythm and key of each example below.
Can you find the fourth intervals?

JH1536

35

Rhythm—Tap the following rhythmic examples.
Count out loud with confidence!

Sight reading—With the metronome set at ♩ = 92, clap or tap the following examples.
Then play these at the same metronome speed. Play with energy!

LESSON DAY

Rhythm—Point to the example that you hear your teacher clap. Listen carefully!
Then count and clap both examples.

Sight reading—Plan ahead: study the key and rhythm of each example below.
Circle the melodic fourths in each example. Play with a steady pulse!

FJH1530

Ensemble Piece

Before you begin this duet, clap and count the rhythm of the student part. Circle all of the melodic and harmonic fourths and play them before you sight read the duet. Keep your eyes on the music and count as you play! Reading the title of the duet, will the piece be slow or fast?

Hot Air Balloon

Teacher accompaniment (student plays one octave higher than written)

? After playing, ask yourself, "Did the piece sound like the title?"

Unit 19

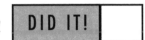

New Concept: melodic fifths

Rhythm—Clap the following rhythmic examples and count. Whisper the rests! **DID IT!**

Sight reading—Tap and count the rhythm.
Play all the fifth intervals before playing the examples as written.

DAY TWO

Rhythm—Draw arrows (up or down) to show the direction of the musical line, and circle each group of repeated notes. Point to each note as you count along. **DID IT!**

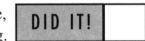

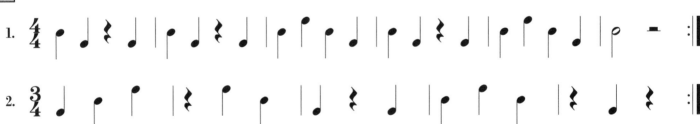

Sight reading—Count the rhythm of these melodies silently while following the music with your eyes. Then play without stopping!

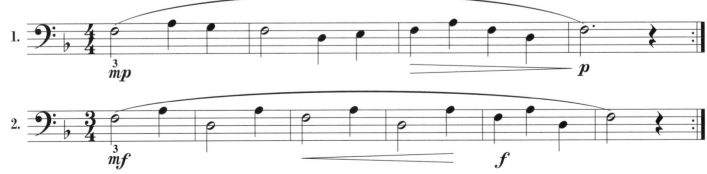

3
DAY THREE

Rhythm—Speak the lyrics in rhythm while you point to each note.

DID IT!

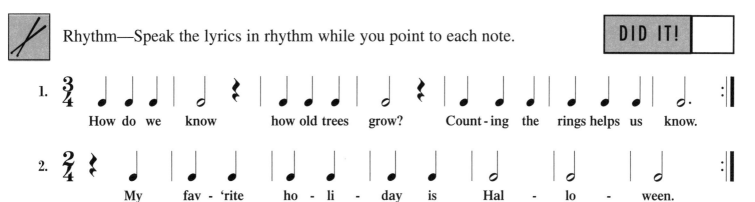

1. How do we know how old trees grow? Count-ing the rings helps us know.

2. My fav-'rite ho - li - day is Hal - lo - ween.

Sight reading—Tap the rhythm before playing.
Set a strong rhythmic pulse and then play without stopping!

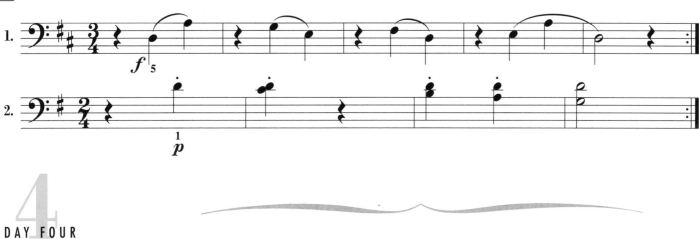

4
DAY FOUR

Rhythm—Add bar lines to the following rhythms.
When you have finished, clap and count each line twice.

DID IT!

Sight reading—Study the rhythm and direction of the moving notes below.
Plan all of the harmonic intervals. Then play each example from beginning to end without stopping!

Rhythm—Tap the following rhythmic examples.
Count loudly with energy in your voice!

DID IT!

Sight reading—Silently play the melodies on the top of the keys at ♩ = 100. Keep a steady beat while you play and listen to the rise and fall of the melody. Try playing them again at a faster speed.

⭐ LESSON DAY

Rhythm—Your teacher will clap one of the following examples. Point to the rhythm you hear your teacher clap. Then choose the other example to clap. Can you clap either example from memory?

Sight reading—Plan the intervals, fingering, and articulations.
Then play each example, listening for a steady pulse!

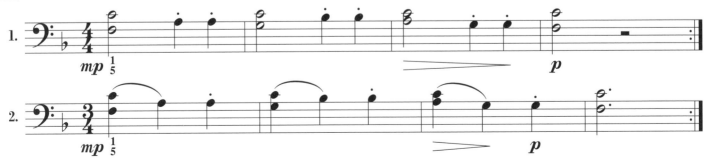

FJH153

 **LESSON DAY**

Ensemble Piece

Before you begin this duet, clap and count the rhythm of the student part, whispering when you count the rests.

Total Eclipse

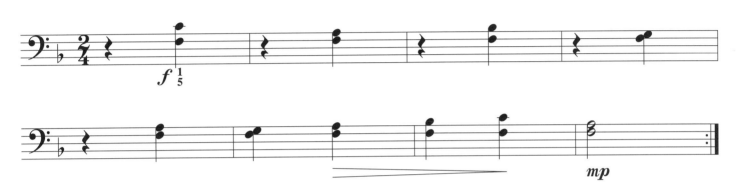

Teacher accompaniment (student plays one octave higher than written)

? After playing, ask yourself, "Did I keep my eyes on the music and keep it steady?"

Unit 20

Review of all concepts

DAY ONE

Rhythm—Clap the following rhythmic examples and count loudly.
When you are counting a rest, whisper.

DID IT!

1.

2.

Sight reading—Tap the rhythm before playing. Circle the C, G (𝄞), or F (𝄢) guide notes.
Then play the melodies without stopping!

DAY TWO

Rhythm—Draw arrows (up or down) to show the direction of the musical line,
and circle each group of repeated notes. Point to each note as you count along.

DID IT!

1.

Sight reading—Look at the first note of both examples and mark the closest guide note
(middle C, bass F, treble G, treble or bass C). Plan the sound and play with a steady pulse!

FJH153

3

Rhythm—Speak the lyrics in rhythm while you point to each note.

DID IT!

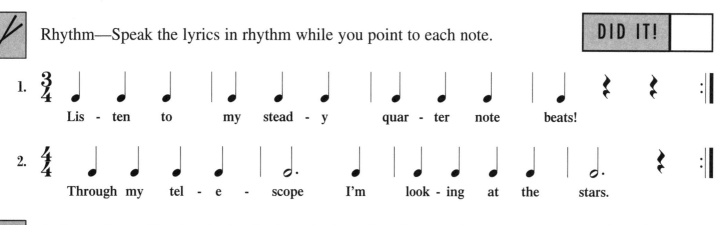

1. Lis - ten to my stead - y quar - ter note beats!

2. Through my tel - e - scope I'm look - ing at the stars.

Sight reading—Tap the rhythm before playing. Play the melody without stopping, observing pitches and rhythm. Plan the dynamics before starting.

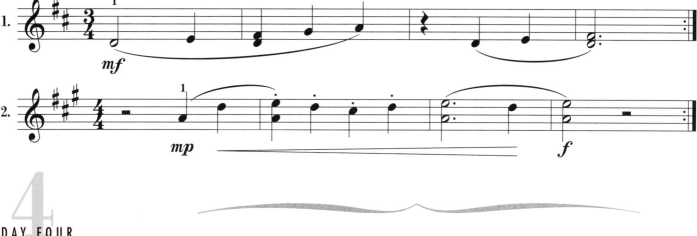

4

Rhythm—Add bar lines to the following rhythms.
Repeat each example, the second time faster and softer than the first.

DID IT!

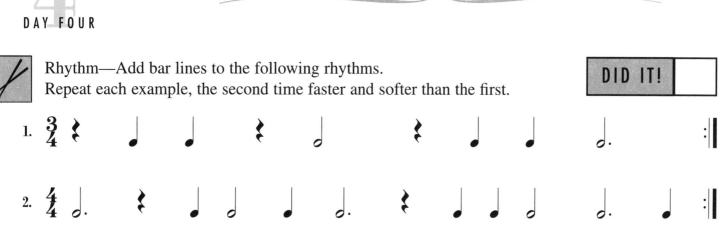

Sight reading—Slowly and silently play each example below on the top of the keys.
Then play as written at a tempo that you can keep steady. Always look ahead!

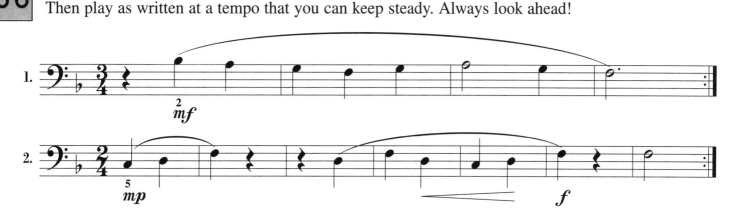

DAY FIVE

 Rhythm—Tap the following rhythmic examples.
Count out loud with confidence!

 Sight reading—Silently play the melodies on the top of the keys at ♩ = 100. Keep a steady beat while you play and listen to the rise and fall of the melody. Try playing them again at a faster speed.

⭐ LESSON DAY

 Rhythm—Clap each example below. For all of the "X" notes, snap your fingers or knock on the wood of the piano!

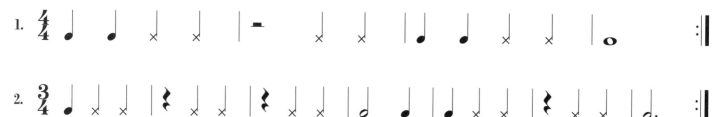

 Sight reading—Circle all of the thirds and fourths in the examples below. Then play, listening for the *staccato* and *legato* articulations.

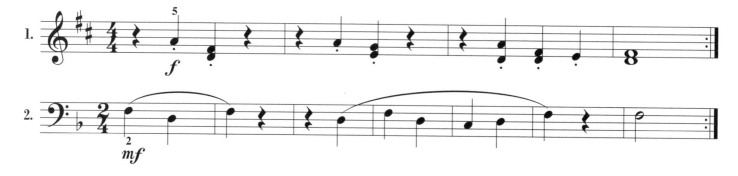

FJH153

Ensemble Piece

DID IT! [ ]

Before you begin this duet, silently play it on the fallboard. Plan ahead: key signature, dynamics, and fingering.

Pirate Attack

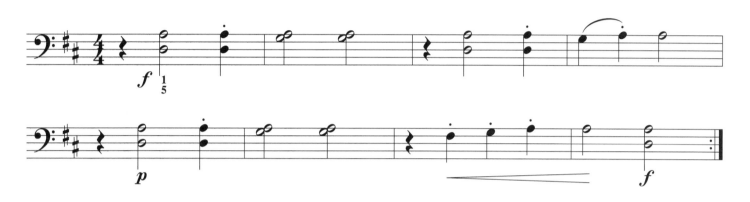

Teacher accompaniment (student plays as written)

? After playing, ask yourself, "Was the piece *f* and strong where it was supposed to be? Did I keep going no matter what?"

Sight Reading and Rhythm Review

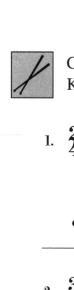 Clap and count the following eight-measure examples out loud. Keep a steady pulse, and don't stop!

1.

2.

3.

4.

 Tap the following four-measure examples out loud, using your right hand for the upstems and your left hand for the downstems. Keep your eyes on the music!

5.

6.

- Play the following harmonic intervals, then write in the intervals you played.
  Example:

3rd

- Circle and label the guide notes. Then write in the intervals.

Example:

C-3rd up

- Fill in the following key signatures.

1 sharp   1 flat   2 sharps   3 sharps

- Play the following two musical examples, following the ⟨ and ⟩ signs.
  Which one is more musical–A or B?

A   *p*

B   *mf*

Additional Sight Reading Exercises

Unit 11: Count out loud while you play.

Unit 12: Keep your eyes on the music and count as you play.

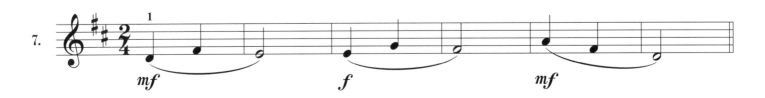

48

Unit 13: Keep your eyes on the music and count as you play.

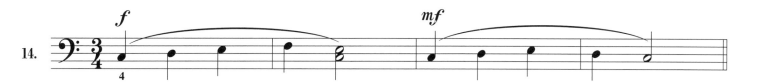

15. *fingering?* ___

Unit 14: Find the harmonic 2nds before playing.

16.

17.

18. *fingering?* ___

19.

20.

Unit 15: Find the harmonic 4ths before playing.

21.

FJH153

Unit 16: Tap the rhythm before playing.

29.

fingering? ___

fingering? ___

30.

31.

32.

Unit 17: Keep your eyes on the music when you play and count.

33.

(move) ①

34.

35.

FJH15

36.

fingering? ___

37.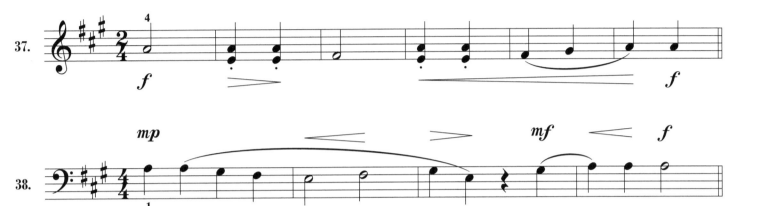

38.

Unit 18: Look through each example before playing.

39.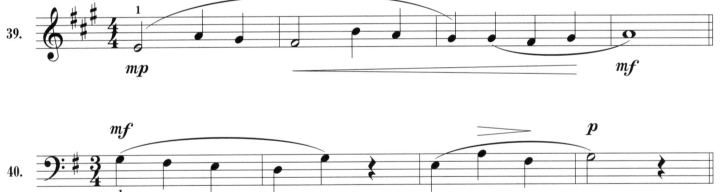

40.

41.

42.

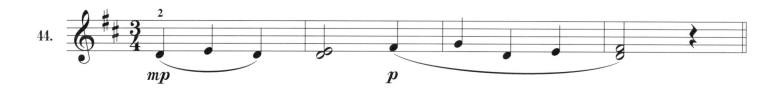

Unit 19: Notice the melodic 5ths before playing.

fingering? ___

fingering? ___

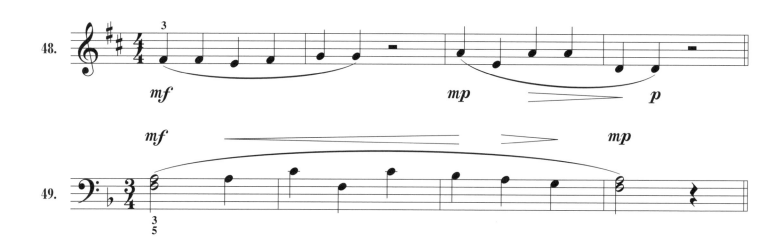

50.

Unit 20: Set a tempo that you can keep steady.

51.

52.

53.

54.

55.

56.

Certificate of Achievement

_____

has successfully completed

SIGHT READING & RHYTHM EVERY DAY®

BOOK 1B

of The FJH Pianist's Curriculum®

You are now ready for **Book 2A**

_____
Date

_____
Teacher's Signature